# Climbing the Corporate Ladder: A Comprehensive Guide to Advancing in Any Workplace

By

Nathan Mann

Table of Contents:

# 1. Introduction

Understanding the dynamics of the modern workplace is crucial for anyone aspiring to climb the corporate ladder. Workplaces are intricate ecosystems, each with its own unique culture, hierarchy, and communication patterns. To navigate this terrain successfully, individuals must grasp the various elements that shape the dynamics of their workplace. Workplace dynamics encompass the interactions, relationships, and power structures within an organization. From the water cooler conversations to boardroom decisions, every aspect plays a role in shaping the overall environment. Hierarchies exist not only on organizational charts but also in informal networks that influence decision-making and career trajectories.

Recognizing the unwritten rules and social norms is as important as understanding the official policies. For instance, knowing who the influential individuals are, understanding the company's tolerance for risk-taking, and being aware of the preferred communication channels can greatly impact one's ability to advance.

Career advancement is more than just climbing a hierarchical ladder; it is a dynamic process of growth and development. In today's competitive work environment, standing still often means falling behind. Advancing in your career is not only about earning promotions but also about acquiring new skills, expanding your network, and achieving personal and professional fulfillment. As organizations evolve, they seek individuals who can adapt and contribute to their growth. Career advancement is a two-way street: while individuals strive to progress in their careers, organizations also benefit from having skilled and motivated employees who can drive innovation and success. A symbiotic relationship forms between personal career goals and organizational objectives. Furthermore, career advancement provides individuals with a sense of purpose and accomplishment. It fosters self-esteem and encourages continuous learning. By setting and achieving career goals, individuals can create a meaningful narrative for their professional lives.

Success in the workplace doesn't happen overnight; it requires strategic planning and intentional actions. Setting the stage for success involves a combination of self-awareness, goal-setting, and understanding the intricacies of the workplace. Here are key steps to lay the foundation for a successful career advancement journey. Before embarking on the journey of climbing the corporate ladder, take the time for introspection. Understand your strengths, weaknesses, values, and aspirations. Reflect on your past experiences and identify patterns of success and areas for improvement. Self-awareness is the cornerstone of personal development and career planning.

Clearly define your short-term and long-term career goals. Goals provide direction and motivation. They serve as a roadmap, guiding your actions and decisions. When setting goals, make them specific, measurable, achievable, relevant, and time-bound (SMART) to increase the likelihood of success. The modern workplace is dynamic, and skills quickly become outdated. Embrace a mindset of continuous learning. Stay informed about industry trends, acquire new skills, and seek opportunities for professional development. This not only enhances your value to the organization but also positions you as a proactive and adaptable professional.

Building a robust professional network is a strategic move for career advancement. Actively engage with colleagues, superiors, and industry peers. Attend networking events, join professional organizations, and utilize online platforms. A strong network provides support, opens doors to opportunities, and enhances your visibility within the organization. Success often lies outside of comfort zones. Be willing to take on challenges and stretch assignments. Demonstrate initiative by proposing new ideas, volunteering for projects, and showing a proactive attitude. Taking calculated risks can set you apart and showcase your potential for growth and leadership.

Your professional reputation is a valuable asset. Cultivate a positive image by consistently delivering high-quality work, demonstrating integrity, and collaborating effectively with others. A positive attitude and strong work ethic contribute significantly to how you are perceived within the organization. Understanding workplace dynamics, recognizing the importance of career advancement, and setting the stage for success are foundational elements for anyone aspiring to climb the corporate ladder. By navigating the intricacies of the workplace, aligning personal goals with organizational objectives, and taking intentional steps toward success, individuals can position themselves for fulfilling and rewarding careers. The subsequent chapters will delve deeper into specific strategies and skills necessary for sustained career advancement.

2.   Understanding the Corporate Landscape

In the intricate world of corporate dynamics, success often hinges on one's ability to navigate the complex terrain of organizational structures, identify key players, grasp company culture, and embrace change with adaptability. This chapter delves into these critical aspects, providing insights and strategies for those seeking to climb the corporate ladder.

Organizations come in various shapes and sizes, each with its unique hierarchy and reporting structures. Navigating this labyrinth is essential for career advancement. Understanding the formal structure helps you identify where decisions are made, who holds the decision-making power, and how information flows within the organization.

## Hierarchical Structures

Traditional hierarchical structures are characterized by clear lines of authority and well-defined roles. Climbing the ladder in such organizations often involves following a predetermined career path. Identifying your position within this structure and understanding the reporting lines can help you determine the most effective channels for communication and collaboration.

## Matrix Structures

In matrix organizations, employees often report to both functional managers and project managers simultaneously. This structure requires adaptability and the ability to collaborate across various departments. Recognizing the nuances of a matrix structure is crucial for leveraging opportunities and building influential networks.

## Flat Organizations

Some modern workplaces adopt a flat organizational structure to promote agility and innovation. In these environments, hierarchies are minimized, and decision-making is decentralized. Advancement may require a different set of skills, focusing on collaboration, initiative, and lateral thinking.

## Tips for Navigating Organizational Structures:

- Study the organizational chart: Familiarize yourself with the company's structure to understand reporting lines and decision-making processes.

- Identify key departments: Recognize the functions of different departments and their roles in achieving organizational goals.

- Build cross-functional relationships: In matrix organizations, connecting with colleagues from various departments enhances your ability to collaborate effectively.

Success in any workplace involves recognizing and understanding the influential figures who shape decisions and drive organizational goals. Identifying key players goes beyond formal titles; it involves recognizing individuals who hold sway, whether due to their expertise, experience, or networking abilities. Executive leadership teams typically consist of C-suite executives responsible for the overall direction of the organization. Understanding their vision and priorities is essential for aligning your career goals with the company's strategic objectives. Not all key players hold official titles. Informal influencers, often found at various levels of the organization, wield significant influence due to their relationships, expertise, or ability to mobilize teams. Building relationships with these influencers can enhance your visibility and open doors to new opportunities.

Identifying mentors within the organization is crucial for personal and professional growth. Mentors offer guidance, share insights, and provide valuable feedback. Look for individuals who have successfully navigated the corporate landscape and express genuine interest in fostering talent.

**Tips for Identifying Key Players:**

- Attend networking events: Actively participate in company-wide events to meet key players from different departments.

- Seek mentorship: Approach experienced professionals for mentorship, and be open to learning from those who have successfully advanced in their careers.

- Stay informed: Regularly update yourself on organizational changes, leadership updates, and industry trends.

Company culture is the collective personality of an organization, encompassing its values, beliefs, and behaviors. Understanding and aligning with the company's culture is vital for career advancement, as it shapes how employees interact, make decisions, and contribute to the overall mission. Identifying the core values that underpin the company culture provides a roadmap for aligning your actions and decisions. Whether it's a focus on innovation, collaboration, or customer-centricity, embodying these values enhances your integration into the organizational fabric.

Different organizations have distinct communication styles, ranging from formal and structured to informal and collaborative. Observing and adapting to the prevailing communication norms helps you convey your ideas effectively and build strong professional relationships. Many companies prioritize diversity and inclusion as integral components of their culture. Recognizing the importance of diverse perspectives and actively participating in inclusive initiatives demonstrates your commitment to the organizational ethos.

**Tips for Grasping Company Culture:**

- Observe and listen: Pay attention to how colleagues interact, the language they use, and the cultural rituals within the organization.

- Embrace diversity: Actively engage with colleagues from diverse backgrounds to foster an inclusive environment.

- Align with values: Integrate the company's values into your work and decision-making to demonstrate cultural alignment.

In today's rapidly evolving business landscape, adaptability is a key factor in career advancement. Embracing change involves being open to new ideas, technologies, and ways of working. Organizations that foster a culture of innovation and change present opportunities for those willing to adapt. Advancements in technology can reshape industries and job functions.

Staying informed about technological trends and acquiring relevant skills positions you as an asset to the organization, especially during periods of digital transformation.

The ability to navigate uncertainty and remain resilient in the face of challenges is highly valued in the workplace. Embracing change requires flexibility and a positive mindset, demonstrating your capacity to contribute constructively during periods of organizational transformation. Adaptability is closely linked to a commitment to continuous learning. Actively seeking opportunities to acquire new skills, attend training programs, and pursue professional development positions you as someone who is not only adaptable but also proactive in personal growth.

**Tips for Embracing Change and Adaptability:**

- Stay informed: Regularly update your knowledge about industry trends, technological advancements, and market changes.

- Embrace a growth mindset: View challenges as opportunities for learning and growth, and encourage others to do the same.

- Seek feedback: Actively seek feedback on your adaptability and willingness to embrace change, and use it to refine your approach.

Understanding the corporate landscape is foundational to a successful career journey. Navigating organizational structures, identifying key players, grasping company culture, and embracing change and adaptability set the stage for future chapters where we'll delve into the skills and strategies needed for continued advancement in any workplace. Remember, success in the corporate world is not only about climbing the ladder but also about building a sturdy foundation that supports your ascent.

## 3. Self-Discovery and Personal Branding

In the intricate tapestry of professional growth, the foundation lies in a deep understanding of oneself. Self-discovery is the compass that guides us through the labyrinth of a career, and personal branding serves as the flag that signifies our unique presence in the workplace. In this chapter, we delve into the transformative journey of self-discovery and the art of crafting a compelling personal brand. Through the exploration of strengths, weaknesses, career goals, and the nurturing of a growth mindset, individuals can not only advance in their careers but also foster a sense of fulfillment in their professional lives.

Before embarking on any journey, it's crucial to assess the tools at your disposal. This holds true for your professional journey as well. Understanding your strengths and weaknesses is not only a means of self-awareness but a strategic move to position yourself effectively in the workplace. Begin with a thorough inventory of your skills, experiences, and attributes. What are the tasks that come naturally to you? In which areas do you consistently excel? These are your strengths, the pillars on which you can build a successful career. Conversely, acknowledging your weaknesses is not a sign of vulnerability but a testament to your honesty and commitment to growth.

Consider feedback from colleagues, superiors, and even subordinates. Constructive criticism is a valuable resource for self-improvement. Are there skills you could refine? Are there aspects of your work that might benefit from additional attention? The goal is not perfection but a continuous journey towards becoming the best version of yourself.

Imagine setting out on a road trip without a destination in mind. You might enjoy the journey, but the chances of reaching a fulfilling endpoint are slim. The same principle applies to your career. Clearly defined goals provide a roadmap, a sense of direction that propels you forward.

Begin by asking yourself fundamental questions. What do you want to achieve in the short term? Where do you see yourself in five, ten, or even twenty years? Define both professional and personal goals, considering aspects like job title, salary, work-life balance, and skills acquisition. Break these long-term aspirations into smaller, actionable steps. Create a timeline and set milestones that will mark your progress. This structured approach not only fuels motivation but also allows for regular reassessment and adjustment as your career evolves.

In an era dominated by information and connectivity, your personal brand is your currency. It's the distinct mark you leave on your professional landscape. Building a personal brand involves aligning your values, skills, and unique qualities to create a memorable and authentic professional identity. Consider the narrative you want to convey. How do you want to be perceived by colleagues, clients, and superiors? What sets you apart from others in your field? Your personal brand is not a facade but a genuine reflection of who you are and what you bring to the table.

Craft a compelling elevator pitch that succinctly communicates your value proposition. This is not just a marketing tool but a guiding statement that reminds you of your worth and goals. Leverage online platforms, such as LinkedIn, to showcase your professional journey, accomplishments, and insights. Consistency is key; ensure your personal brand aligns seamlessly with your actions and contributions in the workplace.

Central to self-discovery and personal branding is the cultivation of a growth mindset. Coined by psychologist Carol S. Dweck, a growth mindset is the belief that abilities and intelligence can be developed through dedication and hard work. Embracing this mindset is transformative, as it opens the door to continuous improvement and resilience in the face of challenges. Challenge the notion that your abilities are fixed. View setbacks not as failures but as opportunities for learning and development. Seek out challenges that push you out of your comfort zone, knowing that the process of overcoming them will lead to personal and professional growth.

Surround yourself with individuals who embody a growth mindset. Learn from their experiences, share your insights, and celebrate collective achievements. As you navigate the dynamic landscape of your career, a growth mindset will not only enhance your adaptability but also foster a culture of innovation and collaboration in your workplace.

Self-discovery and personal branding are not one-time endeavors but ongoing processes that evolve with your career. By consistently assessing your strengths and weaknesses, defining clear career goals, building a genuine personal brand, and cultivating a growth mindset, you lay the groundwork for not only climbing the corporate ladder but for a fulfilling and resilient professional journey. This chapter serves as a compass, guiding you toward the next steps of your career advancement. Embrace the journey of self-discovery and personal branding, and witness the transformation it brings to both your professional and personal life.

## 4. Effective Communication Skills

Communication is the cornerstone of success in any workplace. It's not just about speaking clearly or writing eloquently; it's about understanding the nuances of verbal and non-verbal cues, actively listening to others, and presenting your thoughts with impact. In this chapter, we will delve into the various facets of effective communication and explore how mastering these skills can significantly contribute to your climb up the corporate ladder.

Effective verbal communication begins with clarity. Your words should convey your message without ambiguity. Practice articulating your thoughts in a straightforward manner, avoiding unnecessary jargon or complex language. Be concise but comprehensive, ensuring your audience can easily grasp the key points. The way you speak can greatly influence how your message is received. Pay attention to your tone, pitch, and pace. A confident and measured delivery exudes authority, while a warm and friendly tone fosters a positive atmosphere. Adapt your communication style based on the context, audience, and the nature of your message.

Verbal communication is not just about words; your body language plays a crucial role. Maintain eye contact to convey confidence and attentiveness. Use gestures purposefully to emphasize key points. A strong and open posture can project authority and engagement. Be mindful of your facial expressions, as they can either reinforce or contradict your verbal message.

In the digital age, written communication is ubiquitous. Whether crafting emails, reports, or presentations, clarity and structure are paramount. Organize your thoughts logically, using headings and subheadings to guide your reader. Clearly articulate your main points and support them with relevant details. Poor grammar and punctuation can undermine the professionalism of your written communication. Take the time to proofread your documents, paying attention to grammar rules, spelling, and punctuation. Use tools like grammar-check software to catch errors and enhance the overall quality of your written work. Different situations require different writing styles. Being able to adapt your writing to the context is a valuable skill. Whether you are crafting a formal business proposal, a casual email, or a technical report, tailor your language and tone to suit the expectations of your audience.

Non-verbal communication includes facial expressions, body language, and gestures. Understanding these cues can provide valuable insights into people's thoughts and feelings. Pay attention to the non-verbal signals of others, and be conscious of the messages your own body language is sending. Non-verbal cues can vary significantly across cultures. What may be considered a positive gesture in one culture could be interpreted differently in another. Be aware of cultural differences in non-verbal communication to avoid misunderstandings and foster effective cross-cultural interactions. With the rise of remote work and virtual meetings, non-verbal communication has taken on new dimensions. Mastering the use of video conferencing tools, understanding virtual etiquette, and effectively conveying emotions through a screen are essential skills for the modern workplace.

Active listening is not just hearing; it's about being fully present and engaged in the conversation. Minimize distractions, maintain eye contact, and show genuine interest in what the speaker is saying. Give them your full attention. Clarifying and summarizing what you've heard demonstrates your commitment to understanding the message accurately. Ask questions for clarification and paraphrase key points to confirm your comprehension. This not only reinforces the speaker's message but also prevents miscommunication. Empathy is a powerful aspect of active listening. Put yourself in the speaker's shoes, acknowledge their feelings, and respond empathetically. This fosters a positive and supportive communication environment, strengthening relationships in the workplace.

Effective communication is a multifaceted skill that goes beyond the words you speak or write. Mastering verbal and non-verbal communication, along with active listening techniques, is fundamental to advancing in any workplace. As you hone these skills, you'll find yourself better equipped to navigate complex professional interactions, build strong relationships, and leave a lasting impression on those around you. In the next chapters, we'll explore additional skills and strategies to further enhance your journey up the corporate ladder.

## 5. Developing Leadership Skills

In the dynamic landscape of the modern workplace, leadership skills are not just reserved for those with lofty titles. Regardless of your position, developing and honing these skills is crucial for professional growth and advancement. This chapter delves into the essence of leadership, guiding you through leading by example, motivating and inspiring others, and mastering conflict resolution and decision-making.

Leadership is not about a title or a corner office; it's about influencing others positively and steering a team or organization towards success. At its core, effective leadership involves a combination of vision, integrity, and the ability to guide others through challenges. A leader must have a clear vision of the future. This vision serves as a compass, guiding the team toward common goals. A leader's ability to communicate this vision is paramount, instilling a sense of purpose and direction among team members.

Trust is the foundation of leadership. A leader with integrity, honesty, and consistency gains the trust of their team. Trust fosters an environment where team members feel safe to express ideas, take risks, and collaborate effectively. In today's fast-paced world, adaptability is a key trait of successful leaders. Being open to change and demonstrating resilience in the face of uncertainty sets the tone for the entire team.

The most influential leaders are those who lead by example. Your actions speak louder than words, and as a leader, your behavior sets the standard for your team. Demonstrate a strong work ethic by consistently putting forth your best effort. Whether it's meeting deadlines, going the extra mile, or tackling challenges head-on, your commitment will inspire others to do the same.

Leaders take responsibility for their actions and decisions. Acknowledge mistakes, learn from them, and show accountability. This transparency fosters a culture of responsibility within the team.  Clear and open communication is a cornerstone of leading by example. Actively listen to your team, communicate expectations clearly, and provide constructive feedback. By doing so, you create an environment where communication is valued and practiced by all.

Motivation is the fuel that propels a team toward its goals. As a leader, understanding how to motivate and inspire others is a skill that can elevate both individual and collective performance. Acknowledge the contributions of your team members. Regularly recognize their efforts, whether through public praise, awards, or simple expressions of gratitude. Feeling appreciated enhances morale and fosters a positive work environment.

Inspire your team by setting ambitious yet achievable goals. When individuals see the value and impact of their work, they are more motivated to put in the effort required to meet and exceed expectations. Empower your team members by delegating responsibilities and providing them with the autonomy to make decisions. This not only develops their skills but also instills a sense of ownership and accountability.

Leadership is not without its challenges, and effective leaders must navigate conflicts and make decisions that impact the team and the organization as a whole. Conflicts are inevitable in any workplace. A leader must possess strong conflict resolution skills, promoting open communication and finding collaborative solutions. Addressing conflicts early prevents them from escalating and negatively affecting team dynamics.

Leaders often face tough decisions. Developing the ability to make timely and informed decisions is crucial. Consider all relevant information, consult with key stakeholders when necessary, and be decisive. Indecisiveness can lead to a lack of direction and erode team confidence. Not every decision will lead to success. Embrace failure as an opportunity to learn and improve. Leaders who can adapt and grow from setbacks inspire resilience in their teams.

Leadership skills are essential for anyone aspiring to climb the corporate ladder. Whether you're leading a small team or influencing from within, embodying the essence of leadership, leading by example, motivating others, and mastering conflict resolution and decision-making will set you on a path to success. As you continue to develop these skills, you not only enhance your own career but also contribute to the growth and success of those around you.

## 6. Strategic Networking

In the fast-paced world of corporate environments, strategic networking has emerged as a crucial tool for professionals aiming to climb the corporate ladder. This chapter delves into the intricacies of building meaningful relationships, the benefits of joining professional organizations, the impact of networking events and conferences, and the strategic use of social media for professional growth. Effective networking is not about collecting business cards or connecting with people on LinkedIn. It's about cultivating meaningful relationships that go beyond superficial interactions. Building genuine connections requires authenticity, empathy, and a willingness to invest time in understanding others.

Authenticity is the cornerstone of any meaningful relationship. People appreciate sincerity, and being genuine fosters trust. When networking, be yourself, share your experiences, and listen actively to others. Authentic connections create a foundation for mutual support and collaboration. Understanding the needs and concerns of others is essential in networking. Empathy allows you to connect on a deeper level, showing that you genuinely care about the well-being and success of your colleagues. Remembering details about others and expressing genuine interest in their aspirations builds a strong foundation for a lasting professional relationship.

Building meaningful relationships takes time. Allocate dedicated time in your schedule for networking activities. Attend industry events, schedule coffee meetings, and participate in team-building activities. Invest in relationships not just for immediate gain but for long-term mutual success. Professional organizations provide a structured platform for networking, knowledge sharing, and skill development within a specific industry. Joining these organizations can significantly enhance your professional network and contribute to your career growth.

Research and identify professional organizations related to your industry or field. Whether it's a local association or an international group, being part of such organizations opens doors to networking opportunities, industry trends, and access to a community of like-minded professionals. Joining a professional organization is not just about being a passive member. Actively participate in events, seminars, and workshops. Volunteer for committees or leadership roles to maximize your visibility within the organization. The more actively you engage, the more you stand to gain from the collective knowledge and expertise within the group.

Attending networking events and conferences is an excellent way to expand your professional network, gain industry insights, and stay updated on the latest trends. However, effective networking at these events requires a strategic approach. Before attending an event, set clear goals for what you want to achieve. Identify key individuals you'd like to connect with and research their background. Prepare an elevator pitch that succinctly introduces yourself, your expertise, and your goals. Being well-prepared enhances your confidence and effectiveness during networking opportunities.

During networking events, focus on quality over quantity. Engage in meaningful conversations rather than trying to collect as many business cards as possible. Be an active listener, ask open-ended questions, and showcase your genuine interest in others. Remember to follow up with your new connections promptly to solidify the relationship. In the digital age, social media has become a powerful tool for professional networking. Platforms like LinkedIn, Twitter, and professional forums offer unique opportunities to connect with industry leaders, share insights, and stay updated on industry trends.

LinkedIn is a central hub for professional networking. Ensure your profile is complete, highlighting your skills, achievements, and professional experience. Actively engage with your network by sharing relevant content, participating in discussions, and endorsing your colleagues. Use social media to position yourself as a thought leader in your industry. Share valuable insights, contribute to discussions, and showcase your expertise. Establishing yourself as a credible and knowledgeable professional can attract opportunities and invitations for collaboration.

Participate in online forums and communities related to your field. Engage in discussions, seek advice, and contribute your expertise. Virtual networking can lead to meaningful connections that may translate into real-world opportunities. Strategic networking is a dynamic and multifaceted aspect of career advancement. By building meaningful relationships, leveraging professional organizations, attending networking events, and utilizing social media effectively, professionals can create a robust network that propels them forward in their careers. The ability to navigate and cultivate connections is not only an essential skill but also a strategic advantage in the competitive landscape of the modern workplace.

## 7. Continuous Learning and Skill Development

In the dynamic landscape of today's professional world, the key to sustained success and career advancement lies in a commitment to continuous learning and skill development. As industries evolve, technologies advance, and job roles transform, individuals who actively engage in lifelong learning are better equipped to navigate change and thrive in their careers.

Lifelong learning is not merely a buzzword; it's a fundamental mindset that separates those who merely survive in their careers from those who thrive. The concept involves the ongoing, voluntary, and self-motivated pursuit of knowledge for personal and professional development. It recognizes that learning is not confined to formal education but is a lifelong journey woven into the fabric of one's professional and personal growth.

In the context of career advancement, adopting a mindset of lifelong learning positions individuals to embrace change, seize new opportunities, and stay ahead of industry trends. This approach fosters adaptability, resilience, and a willingness to acquire new skills—an invaluable asset in today's fast-paced and competitive work environment. Continuous learning becomes truly effective when it is purposeful and aligned with one's career goals. Identifying the skills crucial for advancement in a specific industry or role is the first step toward creating a personalized learning roadmap.

Start by conducting a self-assessment. Reflect on your current skill set, strengths, and areas for improvement. Simultaneously, research and analyze industry trends and the evolving demands of your profession. This dual perspective will help you pinpoint the skills that will not only keep you relevant in your current position but also propel you toward your career objectives. For instance, in the technology sector, skills related to artificial intelligence, data analysis, and cybersecurity might be paramount. In marketing, staying abreast of digital marketing trends, content creation, and social media analytics could be crucial. By identifying these skills, you create a blueprint for your continuous learning journey.

While traditional education undoubtedly provides a strong foundation, the learning journey doesn't end with a degree. Pursuing further education, whether through formal degree programs, online courses, or certifications, is a strategic move toward acquiring specialized knowledge and skills. Consider enrolling in courses offered by reputable institutions or industry-recognized certification programs. These can not only deepen your expertise but also serve as tangible proof of your commitment to ongoing professional development. Many organizations value employees who invest in their education, viewing them as assets that bring fresh insights and skills to the workplace. Additionally, explore workshops, seminars, and conferences relevant to your field. These events offer opportunities to learn from experts, network with professionals, and gain exposure to emerging trends and technologies.

In today's hyper-connected world, staying current is not just a choice—it's a necessity. The speed at which industries evolve requires professionals to be proactive in keeping their knowledge up-to-date.

1. **Engage with Industry Publications and Thought Leaders:** Subscribe to industry journals, blogs, and podcasts. Follow thought leaders on social media platforms to stay informed about the latest developments and insights in your field.

2. **Join Professional Associations and Online Communities:** Participate in professional associations or online forums related to your industry. Engaging with peers allows you to share experiences, gain insights, and stay abreast of industry news.

3. **Networking for Learning Opportunities:** Leverage your professional network for learning opportunities. Attend workshops, webinars, and meet-ups to exchange ideas and experiences with others in your field.

4. **Continuous Skill Assessments:** Regularly assess your skill set and identify areas that need improvement. Seek feedback from mentors or colleagues, and use this information to tailor your learning journey.

Remember, the goal is not just to acquire knowledge but to apply it effectively in your role. Continuous learning is not a passive process; it requires an active and intentional approach to stay relevant and excel in the ever-changing landscape of the modern workplace. In the next chapter, we'll delve into another crucial aspect of career advancement: effective time management. Balancing the pursuit of continuous learning with day-to-day responsibilities is a skill in itself, and mastering it is essential for a successful climb up the corporate ladder.

## 8. Effective Time Management

In the fast-paced world of today's workplaces, mastering the art of time management is not just a skill but a necessity for career advancement. In this chapter, we will explore key aspects of effective time management, including prioritizing tasks and responsibilities, setting SMART goals, overcoming procrastination, and achieving a balance between work and personal life.

One of the fundamental principles of time management is the ability to prioritize tasks and responsibilities. It involves distinguishing between what is urgent and what is important, recognizing tasks that contribute directly to your goals, and understanding the impact of each task on your overall productivity. To effectively prioritize, consider the following steps:

### Assessing Task Importance and Urgency

Create a task list and categorize each item based on its importance and urgency. This can be done using a matrix with four quadrants: urgent and important, important but not urgent, urgent but not important, and neither urgent nor important. This matrix helps in identifying tasks that require immediate attention and those that contribute to long-term goals.

### Identifying High-Impact Activities

Focus on tasks that have a significant impact on your career goals. These high-impact activities should align with your job responsibilities, personal development, and organizational objectives. Prioritizing them ensures that you allocate time and energy to tasks that matter most.

### Utilizing Time Management Tools

Embrace technology and tools that aid in prioritization. Project management apps, to-do lists, and time-blocking techniques can enhance your ability to organize and prioritize tasks. Regularly update and reassess your task list to adapt to changing priorities.

### Setting SMART Goals

Time management goes hand in hand with goal setting. Setting Specific, Measurable, Achievable, Relevant, and Time-bound (SMART) goals provides a roadmap for your career progression. Let's break down the components of SMART goals:

### Specific:

Clearly define your goals. Avoid vague objectives and articulate precisely what you want to achieve. Specify the who, what, where, when, and why of your goals to provide a clear direction.

### Measurable:

Establish criteria to measure your progress. This could include quantitative metrics or milestones that indicate your advancement. Measurable goals provide a tangible way to assess your success.

### Achievable:

Ensure your goals are realistic and attainable. While ambition is commendable, setting unattainable goals can lead to frustration. Assess your resources, skills, and time constraints to set achievable objectives.

### Relevant:

Align your goals with your overall career objectives. Each goal should contribute to your professional growth and bring you closer to your desired position. Consider the relevance of your goals within the context of your organization and industry.

### Time-bound:

Set deadlines for achieving your goals. A time-bound framework creates a sense of urgency and helps you stay focused on your objectives. Break down long-term goals into smaller, manageable tasks with specific timelines.

## Overcoming Procrastination

Procrastination can be a significant obstacle to effective time management. Overcoming this tendency is crucial for career advancement. Here are strategies to combat procrastination:

### Understanding the Roots of Procrastination

Reflect on the reasons behind your procrastination. It could be fear of failure, lack of motivation, or feeling overwhelmed. Identifying the root cause helps you address the issue at its source.

### Breaking Tasks into Smaller Steps

Large tasks can be daunting and contribute to procrastination. Break them into smaller, more manageable steps. Tackling one step at a time makes the overall task less overwhelming and increases your sense of accomplishment.

### Utilizing Time-Blocking Techniques

Allocate specific blocks of time to focus on particular tasks. This technique, known as time-blocking, helps in creating a structured schedule. By assigning dedicated time slots to specific activities, you minimize the temptation to procrastinate.

### Setting Realistic Deadlines

Establish realistic deadlines for tasks. Avoid overcommitting yourself, as unrealistic expectations can lead to procrastination. Setting achievable deadlines contributes to a sense of control and motivation.

### Balancing Work and Personal Life

Achieving a balance between work and personal life is a key aspect of maintaining overall well-being and sustained career success. The concept of work-life balance involves managing your time and energy to ensure fulfillment in both professional and personal domains.

### Establishing Boundaries

Clearly define boundaries between work and personal life. Set specific work hours and avoid bringing work-related tasks into personal time. This separation is crucial for maintaining mental and emotional well-being.

**Prioritizing Self-Care**

In the pursuit of career advancement, it's essential not to neglect self-care. Regular exercise, sufficient sleep, and leisure activities contribute to physical and mental health. A healthy, energized individual is more likely to perform well in the workplace.

**Effective Delegation**

Recognize when to delegate tasks. Delegating not only lightens your workload but also allows others to contribute and grow. Effective delegation is a skill that enhances team dynamics and your overall productivity.

**Utilizing Flexible Work Arrangements**

Explore and leverage flexible work arrangements offered by your organization. This could include remote work options, flexible hours, or compressed workweeks. These arrangements can contribute to a healthier work-life balance.

Effective time management is a cornerstone of career advancement. By prioritizing tasks, setting SMART goals, overcoming procrastination, and maintaining a balance between work and personal life, you equip yourself with the tools needed for success. In the next chapter, we will delve into the importance of building a strong work ethic and consistently delivering high-quality results in the workplace.

## 9. Building a Strong Work Ethic

In the competitive landscape of today's workplaces, a strong work ethic stands as a cornerstone for professional success. In this chapter, we delve into the essential components of building a robust work ethic, exploring the significance of consistency, reliability, initiative, taking ownership of projects, and going above and beyond. Consistency and reliability are the bedrock of a strong work ethic. Being consistent in your performance establishes trust among colleagues and supervisors. Consistency doesn't mean maintaining the status quo but rather delivering quality work consistently over time. It involves meeting deadlines, adhering to standards, and ensuring that your work is dependable. Reliability goes hand in hand with consistency. Colleagues and superiors need to rely on you to complete tasks accurately and on time. This reliability builds your reputation as a dependable team member, paving the way for increased responsibilities and opportunities.

*Practical Tip:* Create a schedule that allows you to consistently meet deadlines and fulfill your responsibilities. Utilize project management tools to stay organized and ensure tasks are completed on time.

Initiative is the engine that drives professional growth. Instead of waiting for tasks to be assigned, individuals with a strong work ethic take the initiative to identify opportunities and challenges. They actively seek ways to contribute to the success of their team and the organization as a whole. Demonstrating initiative involves being proactive in identifying areas for improvement, suggesting innovative solutions, and volunteering for projects. It showcases your commitment to the organization's goals and your willingness to go beyond the expected.

*Practical Tip:* Regularly assess your work environment for opportunities to improve processes or contribute in new ways. Present your ideas in a constructive manner, highlighting how they align with the organization's objectives.

Taking ownership of projects goes beyond merely completing assigned tasks. It involves embracing a sense of responsibility and accountability for the success of a project from start to finish. Those with a strong work ethic don't shy away from challenges; instead, they proactively tackle them, taking pride in their work and ensuring its success. Taking ownership also means being solution-oriented. When obstacles arise, individuals with a strong work ethic actively seek solutions rather than placing blame. This mindset not only fosters a positive work environment but also positions you as a reliable and capable team member.

*Practical Tip:* When assigned a project, create a comprehensive plan that outlines key milestones, potential challenges, and strategies for overcoming them. Regularly communicate progress to relevant stakeholders, showcasing your commitment to project success.

Going above and beyond is the hallmark of individuals who are not content with meeting expectations; they strive to exceed them. This involves putting in extra effort to deliver exceptional results and making meaningful contributions beyond the scope of your role. Those who go above and beyond are often recognized for their dedication and commitment. This recognition can lead to increased visibility within the organization, career advancement opportunities, and the trust of colleagues and superiors.

*Practical Tip:* Identify areas where you can add value beyond your regular responsibilities. Volunteer for cross-functional projects, offer to mentor junior colleagues, or propose initiatives that align with the organization's strategic goals.

Building a strong work ethic is not an overnight endeavor; it requires dedication, self-discipline, and a commitment to continuous improvement. Consistency, reliability, initiative, taking ownership of projects, and going above and beyond are the pillars upon which a robust work ethic is built. By embodying these principles, you position yourself as a valuable asset to your organization. As you consistently demonstrate your commitment to excellence, you not only climb the corporate ladder but also inspire those around you to strive for their best. In the next chapter, we explore the crucial role of effective time management in your journey toward professional advancement.

## 10. Navigating Challenges and Overcoming Setbacks

In the journey of climbing the corporate ladder, challenges and setbacks are inevitable companions. Whether you're facing a project gone awry, a missed promotion, or a significant professional hurdle, how you respond to adversity can make all the difference in your career trajectory. This chapter explores the importance of resilience, learning from failure, seeking feedback, and maintaining a positive attitude in the face of challenges. Resilience is the bedrock of a successful career. It's not about avoiding challenges but rather about bouncing back from them stronger than before. Resilient individuals understand that setbacks are not permanent, and they view challenges as opportunities for growth.

**Strategies for Building Resilience:**

1. **Cultivate a Growth Mindset:** Embrace challenges as opportunities to learn and improve. Recognize that setbacks are not a reflection of your abilities but rather stepping stones toward success.

2. **Develop Emotional Intelligence:** Understand and manage your emotions effectively. Emotional intelligence enables you to navigate challenging situations with a clear head, making it easier to bounce back.

3. **Build a Support System:** Surround yourself with a network of supportive colleagues, friends, and mentors. Having a strong support system can provide valuable perspectives and encouragement during tough times.

4. **Practice Self-Care:** Take care of your physical and mental well-being. Regular exercise, adequate sleep, and mindfulness practices contribute to emotional resilience.

Failure is not the end; it's a stepping stone to success. Embracing failure as a natural part of the learning process is crucial for professional growth. The most successful individuals view failure not as a setback but as a necessary experience on the path to mastery.

**Extracting Lessons from Failure:**

1. **Analyzing Root Causes:** When faced with failure, resist the urge to place blame. Instead, analyze the root causes of the failure objectively. This approach allows you to identify areas for improvement.

2. **Iterative Problem-Solving:** Treat each failure as an opportunity for iteration. Use the feedback gathered from the failure to refine your approach and enhance your skills.

3. **Fostering a Culture of Learning:** Encourage a culture of learning within your team or organization. When everyone sees failure as an opportunity to learn and grow, innovation flourishes.

4. **Celebrating Small Wins:** Recognize and celebrate small victories along the way. Acknowledging progress, even in the face of setbacks, reinforces a positive mindset.

Feedback is a powerful tool for personal and professional development. Actively seeking feedback, whether positive or constructive, allows you to gain insights into your strengths and areas for improvement. Continuous improvement is not just a goal but a mindset that propels you forward.

**Effective Feedback Practices:**

1. **Request Specific Feedback:** When seeking feedback, be specific about the aspects you want insights into. This helps you focus on targeted areas for improvement.

2. **Active Listening:** When receiving feedback, practice active listening. Avoid becoming defensive, and instead, consider the feedback objectively. Use it as a foundation for growth.

3. **Feedback Loops:** Establish regular feedback loops with colleagues, mentors, and supervisors. Consistent feedback facilitates ongoing improvement and ensures you stay aligned with organizational goals.

4. **Documenting Progress:** Keep a record of your achievements, feedback received, and goals accomplished. Regularly review this documentation to track your progress and identify areas that require attention.

Positivity is a catalyst for success. A positive attitude not only influences your own mindset but also impacts the people around you. Maintaining optimism during challenging times is a skill that sets high-achievers apart.

**Strategies for Cultivating Positivity:**

1. **Gratitude Practices:** Cultivate a habit of expressing gratitude. Acknowledge and appreciate the positive aspects of your professional journey, even during challenging times.

2. **Visualization Techniques:** Envision success and visualize your goals. This positive visualization can help shift your mindset from dwelling on setbacks to focusing on future accomplishments.

3. **Mindfulness and Stress Reduction:** Incorporate mindfulness practices into your daily routine. Mindfulness reduces stress, enhances focus, and promotes a positive outlook.

4. **Surrounding Yourself with Positivity:** Choose to surround yourself with positive influences. Engage with colleagues, mentors, and friends who uplift and inspire you.

Navigating challenges and overcoming setbacks is an integral part of any successful career journey. Resilience, learning from failure, seeking feedback, and maintaining a positive attitude collectively contribute to your ability to thrive in the face of adversity. As you progress in your career, remember that setbacks are not roadblocks but opportunities for growth. Embrace challenges with a resilient spirit, learn from failures, seek feedback to refine your skills, and maintain a positive attitude to propel yourself toward long-term success in the workplace.

11. Negotiating for Career Advancement

Negotiation is an indispensable skill on the journey to career advancement. Whether you're seeking a higher salary, better opportunities, or a well-deserved promotion, understanding the art of negotiation is crucial. At its core, negotiation involves a give-and-take process where both parties aim to reach a mutually beneficial agreement.

**Key Principles of Negotiation**

- **Preparation:** The foundation of successful negotiation lies in thorough preparation. Understand your value, research industry standards, and anticipate potential objections. Know your priorities and be ready to articulate them clearly.

- **Active Listening:** Pay close attention to the other party's needs and concerns. Active listening fosters better understanding and helps build rapport, creating a more collaborative atmosphere.

- **Flexibility:** Be open to alternative solutions. A rigid stance can hinder progress. Adaptability allows you to explore creative compromises that satisfy both parties.

Establishing a positive relationship with your counterpart is essential for effective negotiation. Building rapport involves trust, respect, and a genuine interest in finding common ground. Begin conversations on a positive note, express appreciation for the other party's perspective, and demonstrate empathy.

When negotiating your salary, understanding your market value is paramount. Research industry benchmarks, consider your experience and skill set, and factor in regional variations. Websites like Glassdoor, Payscale, and industry reports can provide valuable insights. Timing is a critical aspect of salary negotiations. Choose the right moment, preferably after a successful project or positive performance review. Avoid discussing salary during stressful times for the company or immediately after a setback.

Clearly articulate your contributions and achievements. Showcase how your skills have positively impacted the company's success. Provide concrete examples of projects you've led, problems you've solved, or initiatives you've championed. Negotiations often involve compromise. Be prepared to make concessions while ensuring your core needs are met. This collaborative approach fosters a positive working relationship and increases the likelihood of reaching a satisfying agreement.

Negotiating for better opportunities extends beyond salary. It involves advocating for projects, responsibilities, and growth opportunities that align with your career goals. Clearly communicate your aspirations and how they align with the organization's objectives. Engage in open conversations about your performance and areas for improvement. Constructive feedback provides valuable insights into the expectations of your superiors, enabling you to tailor your negotiation strategies effectively. Proposing innovative ideas showcases your commitment to the organization's success. Whether it's suggesting new projects, process improvements, or cost-saving initiatives, presenting well-thought-out proposals positions you as a proactive and valuable team member.

Receiving a job offer is an exciting moment, but it's crucial to evaluate it thoroughly. Consider the entire compensation package, including salary, benefits, bonuses, and any additional perks. Assess the company culture, growth opportunities, and work-life balance. If you receive a counteroffer from your current employer upon presenting a job offer, approach the situation carefully. Consider the reasons behind the counteroffer, evaluate the potential for positive change in your current role, and weigh the long-term implications.

When vying for a promotion, emphasize your accomplishments, leadership skills, and dedication to the company's success. Clearly communicate how your expanded role aligns with organizational objectives and contributes to overall growth. Negotiating for job offers and promotions should align with your long-term career plan. Consider how each opportunity contributes to your professional growth and whether it aligns with your aspirations. Strategic decision-making ensures you're continually progressing toward your ultimate career goals.

Negotiating for career advancement is a skill that evolves with practice and experience. Approach negotiations with confidence, backed by thorough research and a clear understanding of your value. Whether you're negotiating for salary, better opportunities, or promotions, a strategic and collaborative approach can pave the way for a successful career journey. Remember, negotiation is not a one-time event but an ongoing process that contributes to your continuous growth and success in the workplace.

## 12. Mentorship and Sponsorship

In the dynamic and competitive landscape of the corporate world, the guidance and support of experienced individuals can make a significant difference in one's career trajectory. Mentorship and sponsorship are two powerful tools that professionals can leverage to navigate the complexities of the workplace, build meaningful relationships, and propel their careers forward. Mentorship is a symbiotic relationship where a more experienced individual, the mentor, provides guidance, advice, and support to a less experienced individual, the mentee. This relationship goes beyond formal training and education, offering insights into the unwritten rules of the corporate world. The benefits of mentorship are numerous:

### 1. Knowledge Transfer:

Mentors, often seasoned professionals, bring a wealth of experience and industry knowledge. Through regular interactions, mentees gain access to insights and perspectives that can't be found in textbooks or formal training programs.

### 2. Career Development:

Mentors play a crucial role in shaping the career trajectory of their mentees. They provide advice on career goals, help identify growth opportunities, and offer constructive feedback to enhance professional skills.

### 3. Networking Opportunities:

One of the significant advantages of mentorship is the access it provides to the mentor's network. This expanded network can open doors to new opportunities, collaborations, and professional connections that can be instrumental in career advancement.

## Finding and Building Relationships with Mentors

Identifying the right mentor is a pivotal step in leveraging mentorship for career growth. Here's a guide on finding and building relationships with mentors:

### 1. Self-Assessment:

Before seeking a mentor, conduct a self-assessment. Identify your strengths, weaknesses, and areas for growth. Understanding your needs will help you find a mentor whose expertise aligns with your goals.

### 2. Identify Potential Mentors:

Look within your organization, industry, or professional networks for individuals whose achievements and expertise resonate with your career aspirations. Attend industry events, join professional organizations, and participate in networking activities to expand your pool of potential mentors.

### 3. Initiate the Connection:

Approach potential mentors with respect and humility. Craft a concise and compelling introduction that highlights your admiration for their work and expresses your interest in learning from their experiences. Attend seminars, workshops, or company events where you can interact with potential mentors in a natural setting.

### 4. Build a Genuine Relationship:

Mentorship thrives on trust and authenticity. Take the time to build a genuine connection with your mentor. Share your goals, challenges, and successes, and be open to receiving feedback. Actively listen to their insights and show appreciation for their time and guidance.

## Sponsorship and Advocacy in the Workplace

While mentorship focuses on guidance and advice, sponsorship takes it a step further by actively advocating for a mentee's advancement within the organization. A sponsor is someone with influence who is willing to use their position to champion your career. Here's why sponsorship is vital:

### 1. Visibility and Opportunities:

Sponsors actively promote their proteges within the organization, ensuring that their achievements are recognized by key decision-makers. This increased visibility can lead to career-advancing opportunities, such as high-profile projects, promotions, and leadership roles.

### 2. Breaking Barriers:

Sponsorship is particularly beneficial for breaking through organizational barriers. A sponsor can advocate for you in meetings, recommend you for promotions, and help you navigate organizational politics, ultimately accelerating your career progression.

### 3. Building a Sponsorship Relationship:

Building a sponsorship relationship involves showcasing your skills and contributions, gaining the sponsor's trust, and actively seeking their support. Be proactive in keeping your sponsor informed about your achievements and career goals, and demonstrate your commitment to professional development.

### 4. Reciprocal Relationships:

While sponsors invest in their proteges' success, it's essential for the mentee to reciprocate by delivering results, maintaining a strong work ethic, and continually developing their skills. A successful sponsorship relationship is built on mutual trust and shared success.

As your career advances, there comes a point where you have the opportunity to pay it forward and become a mentor to others. This not only contributes to the growth of your industry but also enhances your leadership skills and personal satisfaction. Here's how you can become a mentor:

### 1. Recognize the Impact of Mentorship:

Reflect on the positive influence mentors have had on your career. Acknowledge the impact of mentorship in your professional growth, and consider how you can contribute to the development of others.

## 2. Make Yourself Accessible:

Communicate your willingness to mentor others within your organization or professional network. Attend mentorship programs, industry events, or volunteer to participate in mentoring initiatives.

## 3. Share Your Knowledge and Experience:

As a mentor, share your experiences, insights, and lessons learned. Provide guidance on navigating challenges, setting career goals, and developing essential skills. Encourage your mentees to take ownership of their careers.

## 4. Foster an Inclusive Mentoring Environment:

Be inclusive in your mentoring approach. Consider mentoring individuals from diverse backgrounds, and create an environment where mentees feel comfortable sharing their goals and concerns.

Mentorship and sponsorship are invaluable tools for career advancement, offering a roadmap for both personal and professional growth. Whether you are seeking guidance from a mentor or considering becoming a mentor yourself, these relationships foster a culture of continuous learning, collaboration, and success in the ever-evolving corporate landscape. Embrace the opportunities that mentorship and sponsorship present, and watch as your career climbs to new heights.

## 13. Diversity and Inclusion in the Workplace

In the ever-evolving landscape of the modern workplace, the emphasis on diversity and inclusion has become a pivotal factor in achieving success and fostering innovation. This chapter delves into the intricate facets of cultivating diversity, creating an inclusive work environment, leveraging the unique strengths diversity brings, and addressing challenges within diverse teams.

Diversity encompasses a myriad of dimensions, including but not limited to race, ethnicity, gender, age, sexual orientation, and cultural background. Embracing diversity goes beyond mere acknowledgment; it involves actively seeking, valuing, and integrating differences within the workplace. Research consistently demonstrates that diverse teams yield better results. Differing perspectives and experiences contribute to enhanced problem-solving, creativity, and innovation. Embracing diversity is not just a moral imperative; it is a strategic advantage for organizations looking to thrive in today's globalized and competitive markets.

Creating an inclusive workplace begins with acknowledging and appreciating the uniqueness of each individual. Cultivate a culture that promotes respect, openness, and acceptance. Provide equal opportunities for growth and development, irrespective of differences, fostering an environment where everyone feels valued. Inclusion is the key to unlocking the full potential of diversity. An inclusive work environment goes beyond mere tolerance; it actively seeks to involve every team member, ensuring that their voices are heard and their contributions recognized.

Leadership plays a pivotal role in setting the tone for an inclusive work environment. When leaders actively support diversity and inclusion initiatives, it sends a clear message throughout the organization. This commitment must be reflected in policies, practices, and decision-making processes. Providing diversity and inclusion training to employees helps raise awareness and understanding. Education on unconscious bias, microaggressions, and cultural competence equips individuals with the tools to navigate diverse environments respectfully and effectively.

Review and modify existing policies to ensure they are inclusive. From recruitment and promotions to flexible work arrangements, inclusive policies reinforce the organization's commitment to diversity. Regularly evaluate and update these policies to align with evolving societal norms. A diverse workforce is a wellspring of innovation. By bringing together individuals with varied perspectives, organizations can tackle challenges from multiple angles, leading to more creative and effective solutions.

Create platforms for employees to share their unique perspectives. Foster an environment where different viewpoints are not only welcomed but actively sought. This can be achieved through brainstorming sessions, cross-functional teams, and inclusive decision-making processes. Encourage employees to develop cross-cultural competence. This involves understanding and appreciating the nuances of different cultures, communication styles, and work practices. Cross-cultural competence enhances collaboration and minimizes misunderstandings within diverse teams.

While diversity brings numerous benefits, it also presents challenges that require proactive and strategic approaches to overcome. Recognizing and addressing these challenges is crucial for maximizing the potential of diverse teams. Diverse teams may encounter communication challenges due to language differences, cultural nuances, or varying communication styles. Implement strategies such as clear communication guidelines, language training, and team-building activities to bridge these gaps.

Unconscious bias can manifest in various forms, influencing hiring decisions, project assignments, and performance evaluations. Organizations should implement training programs to raise awareness of unconscious bias and establish processes to mitigate its impact. Differences within diverse teams may lead to conflicts. Implement effective conflict resolution strategies, emphasizing open communication and understanding. A proactive approach to conflict resolution ensures that issues are addressed promptly, fostering a healthy and productive team dynamic.

Embracing diversity and fostering inclusion is not only a moral obligation but a strategic imperative for organizations aiming to succeed in the dynamic modern workplace. By actively promoting diversity, creating an inclusive environment, leveraging differences for innovation, and addressing challenges head-on, workplaces can harness the full potential of their diverse talent pool, propelling themselves toward success and sustainability.

## 14. Preparing for Leadership Roles

Advancing into leadership roles is a significant career milestone that requires intentional planning and strategic positioning. Whether you're eyeing a managerial position or aiming for an executive role, understanding the key steps to position yourself effectively is crucial. Leadership is not solely about managing tasks; it's about inspiring and guiding a team toward a common goal. Before positioning yourself for a leadership role, take the time to understand the specific requirements and expectations of the leadership positions within your organization.

**Action Steps:**

1. **Research Leadership Roles:** Investigate the responsibilities and expectations associated with various leadership positions in your company.

2. **Talk to Current Leaders:** Seek guidance from current leaders within your organization to gain insights into their journeys and the skills required.

Leadership roles demand a unique set of skills, including effective communication, strategic thinking, and decision-making. Invest time and effort into developing these skills through continuous learning and professional development.

**Action Steps:**

1. **Identify Leadership Competencies:** Determine the key competencies required for leadership roles in your industry and organization.

2. **Enroll in Leadership Programs:** Explore leadership development programs, workshops, and courses to enhance your skills.

Even before officially stepping into a leadership position, you can exhibit leadership qualities in your current role. Take initiative, demonstrate accountability, and showcase your ability to inspire and motivate others.

**Action Steps:**

1. **Take on Leadership Projects:** Volunteer for projects that allow you to lead a team or demonstrate your leadership potential.

2. **Lead by Example:** Model the behavior you would expect from a leader, including a strong work ethic and a positive attitude.

Executive presence goes beyond the ability to lead; it involves projecting confidence, credibility, and gravitas. Developing executive presence is a gradual process that combines self-awareness, effective communication, and a polished professional image. Understanding your strengths, weaknesses, and leadership style is foundational to developing executive presence. Self-awareness allows you to play to your strengths while addressing areas that need improvement.

**Action Steps:**

1. **Seek Feedback:** Request feedback from colleagues, mentors, and supervisors to gain insights into how others perceive you.

2. **Assess Your Communication Style:** Understand how you communicate, both verbally and non-verbally, and identify areas for improvement.

Executive presence is closely tied to your ability to communicate confidently and persuasively. Mastering the art of communication involves clarity, active listening, and the ability to convey complex ideas in a straightforward manner.

**Action Steps:**

1. **Communication Skills Training:** Attend workshops or courses focused on enhancing communication skills.

2. **Practice Public Speaking:** Engage in opportunities to speak in public, whether through presentations, meetings, or conferences.

Your professional image contributes significantly to your executive presence. How you present yourself, both online and offline, shapes perceptions and influences career opportunities.

**Action Steps:**

1. **Dress the Part:** Dress professionally and align your attire with the expectations of leadership roles in your industry.

2. **Online Presence:** Ensure your online presence, including social media profiles and professional platforms, reflects a polished and credible image.

Transitioning into leadership involves not only leading yourself but also guiding and inspiring others. Effective leadership is rooted in a combination of interpersonal skills, emotional intelligence, and the ability to make informed decisions. Leadership is fundamentally about relationships. Building strong connections with team members fosters trust, collaboration, and a positive work environment.

**Action Steps:**

1. **Team-Building Activities:** Organize team-building activities to strengthen relationships and improve teamwork.

2. **Active Listening:** Practice active listening to understand the concerns and perspectives of team members.

Emotional intelligence is a critical component of effective leadership. Leaders with high emotional intelligence can navigate interpersonal dynamics, manage conflicts, and inspire others during challenging times.

**Action Steps:**

1. **Self-Reflection:** Continuously reflect on your emotions and how they impact your interactions with others.

2. **Empathy Training:** Explore training or workshops that focus on developing empathy in leadership.

Leaders are often called upon to make tough decisions and solve complex problems. Developing strong decision-making skills involves a combination of critical thinking, analysis, and a willingness to take calculated risks.

**Action Steps:**

1. **Decision-Making Training:** Participate in decision-making workshops or training programs to refine your analytical and decision-making skills.

2. **Case Studies and Simulations:** Engage in case studies or simulations that mimic real-world leadership challenges.

Succession planning is a strategic process that ensures the organization has a pipeline of qualified individuals ready to assume leadership roles. Understanding the importance of succession planning and taking steps to secure your own career longevity is vital for sustained professional growth. Succession planning involves identifying and developing potential leaders within the organization. Actively participate in this process by showcasing your leadership potential and expressing your interest in future leadership roles.

**Action Steps:**

1. **Engage with HR:** Have conversations with the Human Resources department about succession planning and express your interest in leadership development.

2. **Mentorship and Sponsorship:** Seek mentorship and sponsorship from current leaders who can advocate for your inclusion in succession plans.

Career longevity is not just about reaching leadership positions; it's about continuously evolving and adapting to the changing landscape of your industry. Stay proactive in your pursuit of knowledge and skills.

**Action Steps:**

1. **Create a Professional Development Plan:** Outline a plan for continuous learning, skill development, and career growth.

2. **Industry Involvement:** Stay abreast of industry trends and advancements by participating in conferences, workshops, and networking events.

Longevity in your career is contingent on maintaining a healthy work-life balance. Burnout and stress can hinder your ability to perform at your best and jeopardize your long-term career prospects.

**Action Steps:**

1. **Set Boundaries:** Establish clear boundaries between work and personal life to prevent burnout.

2. **Prioritize Self-Care:** Make self-care a priority by incorporating activities that promote physical and mental well-being.

Preparing for leadership roles is a multifaceted journey that involves self-discovery, skill development, and strategic positioning. As you embark on this path, remember that leadership is not just about reaching a position but also about making a positive impact on your team and the organization as a whole. Continue to refine your skills, cultivate your executive presence, and foster strong relationships to ensure a successful transition into leadership roles and a fulfilling, enduring career.

## 15. Conclusion

In the journey of climbing the corporate ladder, reflection serves as a crucial compass, guiding individuals towards continuous growth and sustained success. As we conclude this comprehensive guide to advancing in any workplace, it is paramount to delve into the importance of introspection, the strategies for sustaining growth in the long term, and the unwavering encouragement for perpetual self-improvement.

Reflection is the mirror that unveils the lessons learned, the victories celebrated, and the challenges overcome. Take a moment to look back at the path you've traversed, acknowledging the milestones that mark your progress. Consider the skills you've honed, the relationships you've cultivated, and the wisdom acquired through both triumphs and setbacks.

Reflecting on your advancement journey allows you to:

- **Celebrate Achievements:** Acknowledge your accomplishments, no matter how small. Recognizing your successes reinforces a positive mindset and builds confidence for future endeavors.

- **Learn from Challenges:** Embrace the challenges you encountered as learning opportunities. Reflecting on setbacks provides insights into areas that may require further development and fortifies your resilience.

- **Identify Growth Areas:** Pinpoint areas where you have shown significant improvement and areas that may need more attention. This self-awareness is instrumental in crafting a targeted plan for continued growth.

- **Assess Alignment with Goals:** Ensure that your current trajectory aligns with your long-term career goals. Reflection allows you to recalibrate your path if necessary, ensuring that your efforts are directed towards your desired destination.

Sustaining growth in the long term requires a commitment to continuous learning, adaptability, and a proactive approach to personal and professional development. It is not just about reaching the next rung of the corporate ladder but about laying the groundwork for enduring success. Consider the following strategies for sustaining growth:

- **Lifelong Learning:** The rapidly evolving landscape of the professional world demands a commitment to lifelong learning. Stay informed about industry trends, advancements, and emerging technologies. Attend workshops, conferences, and training programs to stay ahead of the curve.

- **Adaptability:** The ability to adapt to change is a hallmark of successful individuals. Embrace new challenges, technologies, and methodologies with an open mind. This adaptability not only ensures relevance in your current role but positions you as a valuable asset in the face of organizational shifts.

- **Networking Continuously:** Networking is not a one-time activity but a continuous process. Nurture existing professional relationships and actively seek opportunities to expand your network. The connections you build can open doors to mentorship, collaboration, and unforeseen career prospects.

- **Mentorship and Being a Mentor:** Engage in mentorship relationships to glean insights from experienced professionals. Simultaneously, consider taking on a mentorship role yourself. The act of imparting knowledge and guidance not only benefits others but also reinforces and deepens your own understanding.

- **Strategic Goal Setting:** Establish clear and achievable goals that align with your long-term vision. Break down these goals into smaller, manageable tasks. Regularly review and adjust your goals based on your evolving priorities and the dynamics of the professional landscape.

- **Maintaining Work-Life Balance:** Sustained growth requires a holistic approach to well-being. Strive for a healthy work-life balance to prevent burnout and maintain the energy and enthusiasm needed for long-term success.

Continuous improvement is not just a strategy; it is a mindset that propels individuals towards excellence. As you navigate the intricacies of your career, embrace the concept of Kaizen, the Japanese philosophy of continuous improvement. Here's how you can foster a culture of perpetual advancement:

- **Embrace Feedback:** Constructive feedback is a powerful tool for improvement. Seek feedback from peers, mentors, and supervisors. Use it as a roadmap for refining your skills and approaches.

- **Set Stretch Goals:** Challenge yourself with goals that stretch your capabilities. These goals may require you to step outside your comfort zone, fostering growth and resilience in the process.

- **Invest in Personal Development:** Allocate time and resources to your personal and professional development. Attend workshops, pursue certifications, and engage in activities that enhance your skills and knowledge base.

- **Cultivate a Growth Mindset:** Approach challenges with a growth mindset, viewing them as opportunities for learning and improvement. Embrace setbacks as stepping stones toward greater success rather than insurmountable obstacles.

- **Celebrate Progress, Not Just Perfection:** Recognize that perfection is an unattainable standard. Instead, celebrate the progress you make on your journey. Each step forward, no matter how small, contributes to your overall growth.

- **Encourage Others:** A culture of continuous improvement is not confined to individual efforts. Foster a supportive environment within your workplace by encouraging and acknowledging the growth of your colleagues. A rising tide lifts all boats.

Climbing the corporate ladder is not a singular ascent but a dynamic and ongoing expedition. Your advancement journey is a narrative continually shaped by your experiences, choices, and dedication to improvement. As you move forward, remember that the journey is as valuable as the destination. Reflect on your path, sustain your growth, and let the spirit of continuous improvement propel you towards unprecedented heights in your professional endeavors.